NO LONGER PROPERTY
OF ANYTHINK
RANGEVIEW LIBRARY
DISTRICT

Wild About Wheels

EMERGENCY Vehicles

by Melissa Abramovitz

Consulting Editor: Gail Saunders-Smith, PhD

Consultant: Steven Thompson, PhD
Department of Emergency Management
North Dakota State University

CAPSTONE PRESS
a capstone imprint

Pebble Plus is published by Capstone Press,
1710 Roe Crest Drive, North Mankato, Minnesota 56003
www.capstonepub.com

Copyright © 2015 by Capstone Press, a Capstone imprint. All rights reserved. No part of this publication may be reproduced
in whole or in part, or stored in a retrieval system, or transmitted in any form or by any means, electronic, mechanical,
photocopying, recording, or otherwise, without written permission of the publisher.

Library of Congress Cataloging-in-Publication Data
Abramovitz, Melissa, 1954– author.
Emergency vehicles / by Melissa Abramovitz.
     pages cm. — (Pebble plus. Wild about wheels)
Summary: "Simple text and full-color photographs describe eight differerent vehicles used by emergency personnel"— Provided by publisher.
  Audience: Ages 4–8.
  Audience: K to grade 3.
  Includes bibliographical references and index.
  ISBN 978-1-4914-2115-4 (library binding) — ISBN 978-1-4914-2356-1 (ebook PDF)
  1. Emergency vehicles—Juvenile literature. I. Title.
  TL235.8.A27 2015
  629.225—dc23   2014032593

Editorial Credits
Nikki Bruno Clapper, editor; Janet Kusmierski, designer; Tracy Cummins, media researcher; Laura Manthe, production specialist

Photo Credits
Corbis: AP Photo/Ted S. Warren, 13; Dreamstime: Mrdoomits, Cover; Getty Images: AFP PHOTO / GEOFF CADDICK,
19; iStockphotos: Enjoylife2, 17, monkeybusinessimages, 7; Shutterstock: aarrows, Design Element, Brad Sauter, 11, egd,
5, Mikadun, 15, Mike Brake, 9, Stockbyte, 21.

Note to Parents and Teachers

The Wild About Wheels set supports national curriculum standards for science related to engineering
design, forces and interactions, and structure and properties of matter. This book describes and illustrates
emergency vehicles. The images support early readers in understanding the text. The repetition of words
and phrases helps early readers learn new words. This book also introduces early readers to subject-specific
vocabulary words, which are defined in the Glossary section. Early readers may need assistance to read
some words and to use the Table of Contents, Glossary, Read More, Internet Sites, Critical Thinking
Using the Common Core, and Index sections of the book.

Printed in the United States of America in Stevens Point, Wisconsin.
092014   008479WZS1

Table of Contents

Help in a Hurry. 4

Police Patrol. 10

Search and Rescue. 14

Tow Trucks 20

Glossary. 22

Read More. 23

Internet Sites. 23

Critical Thinking
Using the Common Core. 24

Index. 24

Help in a Hurry

Sirens wail! Lights flash!

Watch out as emergency

vehicles hurry to the rescue.

Ambulances rush sick
or hurt people to hospitals.
These vans have wide
back doors. Stretchers and
medics have to fit inside.

Fire trucks carry ladders, hoses, and water pumps. Firefighters use hoses to put out fires. They climb ladders to rescue people up high.

Police Patrol

Police cars are fast because

they have big engines.

Police cars have sirens,

flashing lights, and computers.

SWAT trucks take police officers and their weapons on dangerous missions. The truck's armor protects officers from gunfire.

Search and Rescue

Search-and-rescue

helicopters find people

in hard-to-reach places.

They can take off and land

without a runway.

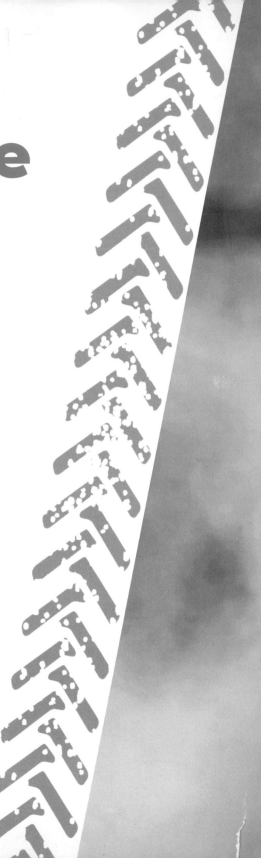

Search-and-rescue boats save lost boaters. They use radar towers and searchlights to find missing boats.

Amphibious responders rescue people on land or in water. These vehicles have wheels and waterproof bottoms.

Tow Trucks

Tow trucks rescue broken vehicles. Flatbed trucks pull vehicles up a ramp. Other tow trucks pull vehicles behind them.

Glossary

ambulance—a vehicle that takes sick or hurt people to hospitals

amphibious responder—a vehicle that runs on land and in water

armor—hard materials that protect people or things

emergency—an event that needs attention right away

medic—someone trained to give medical help in an emergency

mission—a planned job or task

radar—radio signals

stretcher—a thin bed that can be carried to and from an ambulance

SWAT—a team that works in dangerous situations; SWAT stands for special weapons and tactics team

Read More

Arlon, Penelope, and Tory Gordon-Harris. *Emergency Vehicles.* Scholastic Discover More. New York: Scholastic, 2013.

Coppendale, Jean. *Fire Trucks and Rescue Vehicles.* Mighty Machines. Buffalo, N.Y.: Firefly Books, 2010.

Doman, Mary Kate. *Rescue Vehicles.* All About Big Machines. Berkeley Heights, N.J.: Enslow Publishers, 2012.

Internet Sites

FactHound offers a safe, fun way to find Internet sites related to this book. All of the sites on FactHound have been researched by our staff.

Here's all you do:

Visit *www.facthound.com*

Type in this code: 9781491421154

 Check out projects, games and lots more at **www.capstonekids.com**

Critical Thinking Using the Common Core

1. What does a search-and-rescue vehicle do? (Key Ideas and Details)

2. Look at the pictures. How are police cars and ambulances alike and different? (Integration of Knowledge and Ideas)

Index

ambulances, 6
amphibious responders, 18
armor, 12
fire trucks, 8
flatbed trucks, 20
lights, 4, 10, 16
police cars, 10
radar, 16

rescue, 4, 8, 14, 16, 18, 20
search-and-rescue boats, 16
search-and-rescue helicopters, 14
sirens, 4, 10
stretchers, 6
SWAT trucks, 12
tow trucks, 20
workers, 6, 8, 12

Word Count: 158
Grade: 1
Early-Intervention Level: 19